30 Days to Life

The Adventure Begins

A.J. & Cathy Dummitt
Joshua & Jessica Cooper

with Inspiration from Todd Smith
40 Days – A Journey Toward A Deeper Relationship with Christ

TABLE of CONTENTS

(Table of Contents Continued on Next Page...)

READ THIS FIRST!

Welcome to the greatest 30 days of your life so far!

Whether you have recently made the decision to follow Jesus, or you have been a believer for many years, this study book is for you. At times, we all have questions, concerns or even apprehensions regarding our Christian walk. This study was designed to establish basic truths, answer questions and set you on a steady course in your adventure with God. The Christian life is a life of constant growing, maturing and developing. Believe me, no one has "arrived."

Please know, there is nothing you could do to cause Jesus to love you any more than he does right now! We do not follow Him, study His Word, pray or even serve Him in order to gain His acceptance. God told Jeremiah He had set him aside for a special purpose long before he was even born. The same holds true for you! So, relax and realize now that you are not striving for His acceptance or attention. Rest assured, you've got His attention.

Allow your heart to simply enjoy building and enhancing your relationship with Him because He wants you to, not because you have to. Understand an important fact, your relationship with Jesus is the most important one you have. Take it seriously and commit to be faithful in your pursuit of Him. Just as any person would expect his/her spouse to be completely faithful in a covenant relationship, God expects faithfulness as well.

This book is called Thirty Days to Life for a reason. We would suggest you do one day, each day for six days, Monday through Saturday and attend church on Sunday. Meet with the person who gave you this book each week and make it a priority to discuss it with them. In five weeks (thirty days) you will be well on your way to experiencing life on a whole new level. You will be able to understand more clearly the life God intends for you have - the very best life!

May God bless you as you read and study His Word and meet weekly with your study partner to discuss your experiences and these valuable truths.

Week 1 - ME & GOD
(Days 1-6)

Below are some activities that will enhance your new walk with Christ. When you complete the below assignments, check the appropriate box.

☐ Memory Verse - Philippians 4:13

"I can do all things through Christ who strengthens me." (NKJV)

☐ Church Attendance

Church attended _____

☐ Find a Prayer Partner

☐ Prayer Requests

_____

_____

_____

THE NEW ME

When you give your heart to Jesus completely, He gives you a brand new heart. The new heart is full of love for Him and for others. The Bible talks about being "born again" or baptized in the Water, and baptized in the Holy Spirit. When this takes place, God places this new heart inside you and gives you a brand new future. This new life can be an adjustment to say the least, but don't worry, God is going to be with you every step of the way. By reading scriptures and completing the questions below you will gain the confidence you need to make your first steps as a brand new person in Jesus Christ.

*"Therefore if any person is [ingrafted] in Christ (the Messiah) he is a new creation (a new creature altogether); the old [previous moral and spiritual condition] has passed away. Behold, the **FRESH** and **NEW** has come!"* **2 Corinthians 5:17 (Amplified)**

Now that you are a Christian you can expect your life to change.

1. Look carefully at 2 Corinthians 5:17. What happens when you enter into a relationship with Christ?

    _____

2. Read Ephesians 2:1-5.

    a. What was your spiritual condition before you were saved? (vv.1,5)

3

_____

    b. Now what is your condition? (vv.1,5)

_____

3. What are the biggest changes you have noticed in your life since giving your heart to Jesus?

_____

_____

_____

"God loves you just the way you are, but He refuses to leave you that way."
Max Lucado

4. What happened to your previous lifestyle? 2 Corinthians 5:17, Romans 6:6

_____

_____

5. How should one walk after he/she is baptized? Romans 6:4

_____

_____

6. Read Philippians 3:13-14.

    a. According to Philippians 3, what should our mindset be toward things in the past?

    _____

    _____

    b. With this thought in mind, what should you be doing now?

    _____

    _____

7. What are you now? Galatians 3:26

_____

REFLECTION:
Spend the next few minutes in prayer, thanking God for your new life in Him.

GOD 101

Jesus desires to reveal Himself to us a little more each day. His goodness, grace and beauty are beyond our finite comprehension. Think about it. The God of heaven, the Creator of all the universe, desires to know me and have a relationship with me...wow! What a concept! What a privilege! This chapter attempts to get you acquainted with the God that loves you and saved you. Be prepared to be wowed and dazzled by who He is!

1. What do these scriptures teach about God?

Psalm 90:2

_____

_____

Isaiah 40:28

_____

_____

I John 3:20

_____

_____

2. In Psalm 46:1 God is described as:

3. My _____

4. My _____

5. My _____

7

3. Match the statements with the correct verse.

_____ Hebrews 13:5   a. I am the resurrection

_____ John 8:12   b. I am the first and the last

_____ John 11:25   c. I will never leave you

_____ Revelation 1:11   d. There is nothing too hard

                                     for God

_____ Jeremiah 32:17   e. I am the light of the world

4. According to 1 John 4:8, "God is _____."

5. What does Jeremiah 31:3 mean to you?

     _____

     _____

     _____

1. Examine John 3:16. According to this verse, why did God give?

     _____

     _____

     _____

2. Read Acts 17:24. What does this verse say about God?

_____

_____

3. What is God's attitude toward us? 2 Peter 3:9

_____

_____

4. Examine Deuteronomy 7:9. What does this reveal about God's nature and character?

_____

_____

_____

5. In 1 Peter 1:15,16 God gives us a command and why should we obey it?

_____

_____

_____

HOW GOD SEES ME

Throughout the entire Bible we are given glimpses of how God views humanity. In order to have a great relationship with Him, we need to understand how God sees us. From the beginning of time God has had you on His mind. In fact, He is "crazy about you!" You are the apple of His eye. In Zephaniah 3:17 the Bible says, "He rejoices over you with singing." He is not your enemy. He is your friend. The scriptures below take a close look at the Father's heart. Enjoy.

1. In Psalm 139:13-16 David describes God's role in your creation.

    a. (v. 13) What did God do?

    _____

    _____

    b. (v. 14) How are we made?

    _____

    _____

    c. (v. 15) How were you "put together?"

    _____

    _____

2. Read Psalm 139:17,18. Put these two verses in

your own words.

  a. (v. 17)

  _____

  _____

  b. (v. 18)

  _____

  _____

3. Read Romans 5:8. How does God show His love for us (and the world)?

  _____

  _____

4. According to Jeremiah 29:11, God is thinking about you.
What is God *not* thinking about doing to you?

  _____

What is God thinking about you?

  _____

  _____

5. Look closely at Romans 8:38-39. What can separate you from the love of Christ?

_____

6. In Zephaniah 3:17 list five proactive and positive actions of God on your behalf. List them below.

"The LORD your God is with you, he is mighty to save. He will take great delight in you, he will quiet you with his love, he will rejoice over you with singing." (Zeph. 3:17 NIV)

a. _____

b. _____

c. _____

d. _____

e. _____

7. How does Romans 5:8 prove God's love to you?

_____

_____

8. According to Jeremiah 31:3, is God's love for you based upon your behavior?

_____ yes _____ no.

Describe in your own words what this verse means to you.

_____

_____

GOD WANTS TO TALK TO ME

Your relationship with God will continue to get stronger the more you communicate with Him. He wants to hear from you about everything, big or small. When you communicate with God about things in your life, you get His perspective about them. Just praying about things will give you peace and place them into God's capable hands. It is a great privilege to be able to talk to God in a personal way. Remember, the more you pray the more God moves on your behalf. Stay faithful to His Word and seek His face.

1. Read Jeremiah 33:3 carefully and answer the following:

   a. What does God want us to do?

   _____

   b. What will be the end result?

   _____

2. In Psalm 34:4 David prayed. What was the outcome?

   a. _____

   b. _____

3. Look closely at Hebrews 4:16.

   a. What is God's desire for us?

15

_____

_____

b. Why?

_____

_____

4. Who helps us when we pray? Romans 8:26-27

_____

5. Take a thorough look at Philippians 4:6-7.

   What are you encouraged to do about your life
   and the situations you face? (v. 6)

_____

_____

_____

   In your own words, what does verse 7 mean to
   you?

_____

_____

_____

6. What are we instructed to do when praying? Mark 11:23-24

_____

   a. What is God's promise?

   _____

7. Why is it important to forgive others? Mark 11:25-26

_____

8. According to John 15:7, Jesus tells us that two things are necessary in order to receive answers to our prayers. What are they?

   a. _____

   b. _____

9. In whose name must we pray? John 16:24

_____

10. Examine 1 John 5:14-15.

   a. How must we pray? (v. 14)

   _____

   b. What will guarantee that God will hear your

prayers?

_____

c. How should this help you when you pray? (vv. 14,15)

_____

_____

11. Read Ephesians 3:20. In your own words, what is God able to do when we pray in faith?

_____

_____

_____

- *Give thanks to God for the wonderful privilege of prayer.*

- *You can touch God and bring your needs to Him.*

- *Think about it. Your prayers can move the hands that move the world.*

- *Take a few minutes to make a small list of things you will thank God for, and another list of things you would like to ask God to do. (This will keep you focused in prayer).*

- *Go ahead and spend some special time talking with Jesus.*

Thank You God For:

_____

_____

_____

_____

Things I will ask God to do:

_____

_____

_____

_____

Where there is much prayer, there is much power; where there is little prayer, there is little power; where there is no prayer, there is no power.

19

ME AND MY BIBLE

You can treat your Bible as God's Word for your life. Inside you will find principles and concepts that if applied to your life will cause you to be blessed beyond measure. The Bible is a road map for life, and if used properly can prevent many wrong turns and detours leading you further from God. Without this guide we are lost. With an understanding of God's Word we can proceed with surety and certainty, knowing our eternal destination. Take the time every day to allow the Bible to guide your steps.

"Your word is a lamp to my feet
and a light to my path."
Psalm 119:105 (NKJV)

1. How was the Word of God written? 2 Timothy 3:16

_____

2. Read 1 Peter 2:2 carefully and, in your own words, write what this means to you.

_____

_____

_____

3. What will help you understand the Bible? 1 Corinthians 2:12-13

_____

4. Research these scriptures and list what the Bible reveals about its purpose.

Hebrews 4:12 _____

Psalm 12:6 _____

Psalm 119:105 _____

Ephesians 6:17 _____

5. List the four reasons why the Bible is profitable. (2 Timothy 3:16)

Profitable for _____ (teaches you *What's Right*)

Profitable for _____ (teaches you *What's Not Right*)

Profitable for _____ (teaches you *How to Get Right*)

Profitable for _____ (teaches you *How to Stay Right*)

> *"The Bible is the best book in the world. It contains more...than all the libraries I have seen."* John Adams, second President of the United States

6. In your own words, why is it important to read the Bible every day? 2 Timothy 3:17

_____

_____

_____

7. James 1:22 gives us a strong warning. What is it?

_____

8. What is a man like who reads the Word of God and fails to obey it? James 1:23-24

_____

"A Bible that is falling apart probably belongs to someone who isn't"
Christian Johnson

9. What does the Bible say will happen to the person who obeys the Word of God?

a. James 1:25 _____

b. Psalm 1:1-3 _____

c. Joshua 1:8 _____

10. As a Christian, it is impossible to please God without faith (Hebrews 11:6), According to Romans 10:17, how does one build his/her faith?

_____

11. Colossians 3:16 says, "Let the word of Christ dwell in you richly...." The word "dwell" means to inhabit, to occupy, to reside in." List four ways you can cause the Word of God to live inside you.

a. _____

b. _____

c. _____

d. _____

Plan to begin each day with the Word of God.

- *Pray right now and ask God to speak to you from His Word.*

- *Ask Him for the strength to obey His Word.*

- *Thank Him for His words of life that is food for your spirit.*

"I believe the Bible is the best gift God has ever given to man."
Abraham Lincoln, 16th President of the United States

DEALING WITH MY PAST

At some point, everyone has to deal with the mistakes of their past. Choosing to avoid this step will invite trouble into your present and future. Many people suffer from depression, anxiety and stress over things in their past. In fact, some people are even suicidal. The good news is that Jesus has the power, ability and authority to break the chains of regret off your life. There is no sin that He cannot and will not forgive. This chapter will help you to accept His forgiveness.

1. Look up the word "forgive" in a dictionary.

    _____

    _____

    _____

2. Put Psalm 86:5 in your own words.

    _____

    _____

    _____

    _____

3. When you came to Jesus He forgave your sins. According to Micah 7:19, what does God say He did with them?

_____

_____

_____

4. Also, Psalm 103:10-12 gives us insight on how God deals with our sins. What does this verse tell us about our past?

_____

_____

_____

_____

5. Read Romans 5:6-11 carefully.

   a. According to these verses, when did Christ die for us?

   (v. 6) _____

   (v. 8) _____

   (v. 10) _____

   b. Read verse 9 again. Now define "justify" from a dictionary.

_____

c. How are you viewed by God according to the above verses and definition?

_____

_____

_____

6. Read Isaiah 1:18. Describe what God does to us and our sins when we get saved?

_____

_____

_____

"If God forgives us, we must forgive ourselves. Otherwise it is almost like setting up ourselves as a higher tribunal than Him."
C.S. Lewis

7. What did Paul do in order to overcome his past? Philippians 3:13

_____

_____

_____

_____

8. How can you apply the above verse to your life?

_____

_____

_____

9. Read 2 Corinthians 5:17.

   a. What do you think Paul meant by "old things?"

   _____

   _____

   b. What should we be doing now?

   _____

   _____

   _____

10. Think carefully about 1 John 1:9. How does admitting that we have sinned relate to being forgiven?

_____

_____

_____

- *Thank God right now for His grace and mercy.*

- *Praise Him because all of your past failures and sins are forgiven!*

Week 2 - GOD HAS A PLAN FOR ME
(Days 7-12)

CONGRATULATIONS! You just completed your first week in the journey. Continue on your pilgrimage. Complete the assignment below and check the appropriate box.

☐ Memory Verse - Acts 1:8

"But you shall receive power when the Holy Spirit has come upon you; and you shall be witnesses to Me in Jerusalem, and in all Judea and Samaria, and to the end of the earth." (NKJV)

☐ Church Attendance

Church attended _____

How many times church attended _____

☐ Name of Prayer Partner _____

☐ Prayer Requests

_____

_____

_____

☐ Answered Prayers

_____

_____

CAN I KNOW I'M SAVED?

The great news to the question posed in the title is YES! Many people doubt their salvation and they are not quite sure what to do about it. Some people who attend church regularly constantly wonder if they would make it to heaven if they died. There is no reason to live in a state of fear and confusion. The Bible tells us in 1 Corinthians 14:33 that "God is not the author of confusion." God never intended for you to doubt your salvation experience. If you are struggling with anxiety about your experience with God, after this study you will no longer wonder about it. Most importantly you need to know and remember that Jesus loves you and you are His child.

1. What must one do to enter the Kingdom of God? John 3:3,5

   _____

   _____

2. Being saved is not just about saying a prayer, signing a card, or simply believing in your mind that Jesus is the Son of God. The Apostle Peter in Acts 2:38 outlines clearly the steps to salvation. List and fill in the blanks below:

   a. _____

   b. "Be _____, every one

      of you, in the _____ of

_____ for the

_____ of sins"

  c. "you shall receive the _____

     of the Holy Spirit"

3. Look up the word "Repentance" in the dictionary. Write the definition below and describe why this is important.

_____

4. Look at Romans 10:10. What is the result of you believing in Jesus?

_____

5. Read Romans 10:13. In light of questions 1 and 2, explain how, 'calling on the name of the Lord' according to Romans 10:13 applies to these scriptures?

_____

_____

_____

6. What does John 6:47 promise to those who believe?

_____

_____

7. Write down the location, date, and age when you repented, received the Holy Ghost, and were baptized in Jesus name, It is ok if you can't remember the exact date. The date is not what is important, but rather the experience.

_____

_____

_____

_____

8. If we "believe" according to John 7:37-39 what will be the result?

_____

_____

_____

_____

9. How do the following verses help us to realize that we truly KNOW Christ as our Savior?

1 John 4:13

_____

_____

Romans 8:16-17

10. What does 1 John 5:12 mean?

11. What helps us to know we have eternal life? 1 John 5:13

12. According to 2 Corinthians 5:17, what are the results and added benefits of salvation?

GOD'S PLAN FOR ME

Isn't it comforting to know there is a perfect plan for life? When you choose to follow Jesus, and you begin to study His Word, you will realize He has great things planned for you. You can know that you are saved, but there is so much more to God's plan for you than just salvation. In the Gospel of John we read that Jesus came so that we could have life and life more abundant. In order to live this life abundantly we are going to follow the steps found in God's Word and allow the Holy Spirit to lead us daily!

1. What does Acts 2:38 tell us needs to happen in order to start this relationship with Jesus Christ?

   _____

   _____

   _____

2. Have you already...

   Repented of your sins (turned away from that life to go God's direction)?

   ☐ YES   ☐ NO

   Been baptized in water in the name of Jesus Christ (not just in the titles Father, Son and Holy Spirit)?

   ☐ YES   ☐ NO

37

Received the gift of the Holy Ghost with the outward sign of speaking in a language that you hadn't learned before?

☐ YES   ☐ NO

3. In the next few days we will cover the topics above in detail. No matter what your answers are above, be encouraged to keep moving forward with Jesus. Whether you have already completed the initial steps of salvation or not, there is so much more to living for God, and you owe it to yourself to discover it. If there is one area of your life that seems really out of whack spiritually or emotionally right now, write it here:

_____

_____

4. What would an abundant life look like for you?

_____

_____

_____

5. Will you make a commitment to finish this study
    book and allow God to reveal His plan to you for
    an abundant life?

    ☐ YES   ☐ NO

6. What have you learned so far that let's you know
    your life is about to get better?

    _____

    _____

    _____

    _____

MOVING IN THE RIGHT DIRECTION

No matter where you find yourself in your relationship with God right now, the important thing is that you are moving toward Him every day. God is not nearly as concerned with your location as He is with your direction. Every day is a new opportunity to get closer to God and allow Him to lead and guide you into becoming more like Him. Moving in the right direction means you are moving away from sin and things that displease God. As you take steps towards God, He is also moving closer to you as His Word says in James 4:8. Keep moving in the right direction no matter what comes against you!

1. Read Philippians 3:12-14. What great instructions does this verse give us?

   _____

   _____

2. What does Jesus say He is in John 14:6, and why is that important for you?

   _____

3. 2 Timothy 3:16 tells us where we should get our direction, how have you received direction from the Word of God?

41

_____

_____

4. Reading Genesis 19:26 you will find that Lot's wife turned into a pillar of _____. Then in Luke 17:32, we are told to do what?

_____

5. If we are too attached to things in this world, we will miss out on the great things that God has for us. How will remembering Lot's wife help us in our walk with God?

_____

_____

6. Along with the Word of God, who else can help you grow spiritually? (see Ephesians 4:11-12)

_____

_____

_____

_____

7. Romans 12:2 tells us not to be _____,
   but to be _____ by the renewing of
   our minds. WHY?

   _____

   _____

The devil doesn't have to defeat you, he just needs to distract you in order to keep you from being who you are supposed to be in God. Many people get easily frustrated because they are not where they know they should be. Remember, God is not nearly as concerned with your location as He is with your direction. Be encouraged to move in the right direction with God every day. Don't beat yourself up if you aren't where you want to be, but ask a spiritual friend or leader to partner with you in prayer. Keep moving forward, don't stop now.

I find the great thing in this world is not so much where we stand, as in what direction we are moving: To reach the port of heaven, we must sail sometimes with the wind and sometimes against it - but we must sail, and not drift, nor lie at anchor.
-- Oliver Wendell Holmes, Sr.

READY FOR BURIAL

Each follower of Christ must make a commitment to follow Him fully. One key element of salvation is being obedient to His Word by being water baptized in Jesus' name. When we are baptized, the scripture tells us that we are fulfilling the Gospel's plan for burial with Jesus Christ spiritually (Romans 6:4). There is nothing more beautiful than seeing a new believer get water baptized. In this study you will understand its purpose and meaning.

1. What one event launched Jesus into His earthly ministry? Luke 3:21-23

_____

_____

2. According to this example, what should follow immediately after you believe and repent of your sins? Acts 8:36-38

_____

3. In Matthew 28:19,20 the "Great Commission" Jesus gives us and the church as a whole a three-fold assignment. List below.

   a. (v. 19) _____

   b. (v. 19) _____

   c. (v. 20) _____

4. According to Mark 16:16, what should a person do before he/she is baptized?

_____

5. In Luke 24:47 what did Jesus say would be

preached? _____ and

_____ in His

_____

6. Read Acts 10:44-48. What question did Peter ask after the conversion of Cornelius?

_____

_____

_____

7. After Paul and Silas were freed from prison (Acts 16:25-34) they preached the gospel to the jailer and his household. What happened in verse 33?

_____

8. The Apostle Peter spoke clearly on the importance of Baptism in Acts 2:38. This is a critical component in the salvation experience. Please read Acts 2:38 now and write the verse below and circle the word baptized.

_____

_____

_____

_____

_____

9. According to Acts 2:38 why do you think it is important to be baptized with water?

_____

_____

_____

_____

10. Please read the following verses: Acts 2:38; Acts 8:16; Acts 10:48; and Acts 19:5. According to these scriptures in whose name are we to be baptized?

_____

11. Read Romans 6:1-4.

a. What happened to the "old you" when you became born again?

_____

b. Now how should you walk?

_____

TWO FACTS FROM SCRIPTURE:
1. *Jesus places a high priority on baptism.*
2. *Baptism is an essential component of salvation.*

WHAT IS THE HOLY SPIRIT?

God is never going to leave you or walk out on you. He will never turn His back on you (Hebrews 13:5). God truly wants to be your constant companion and be good to you every day. He accomplishes this by placing His Spirit inside of you. He loves you so much that He wants to fill you with His Holy Spirit. What exactly is the Holy Spirit? How will you know when you "have" the Holy Spirit? After reading through the scriptures listed below, many of your questions about the Holy Spirit will be answered directly from the Bible. For the questions that remain, be sure to discuss them with the person who gave you this book.

1. Jesus promised his disciples they would receive a special gift in John 14:16, and 26. Describe that gift from the scriptures.

    _____

    _____

    _____

2. According to Romans 8:9-11, how does a person know if they belong to Christ?

    _____

3. What are some of the benefits of having the Holy Spirit in your life? (2 Timothy 1:7)

    _____

49

4. Before you started this study, what did you understand the Holy Spirit to be?

_____

5. Jesus in His last words to His disciples in Acts 1:4-5 tells them to wait for the _____ of the Father, and that they will be baptized with the _____ _____ not many days hence!

6. Read Acts 1:8. What will you receive after the Holy Ghost comes upon you?

_____

So far, we understand that the Holy Ghost is the Spirit of God, the promise to all who would receive it. Now let's look at the Spirit being poured out in Acts 2.

7. When the people in Acts 2:4 were filled with the Holy Ghost, what happened?

_____

8. According to Acts 2:39, who is the promise of the Holy Ghost for?

_____

_____

9. In Acts 2:38 Peter gave what instructions to those who asked what they needed to do in verse 37?

_____ and be _____

10. What would people receive if they obeyed the first part of Acts 2:38?

_____

11. In Acts 4:31, what happened after they were filled with the Holy Ghost?

_____

"God commands us to be filled with the Spirit, and if we are not filled, it's because we are living beneath our privileges."
Dwight L. Moody

THE HOLY SPIRIT IN ME

Now that we know what the Holy Spirit is - God's Spirit living on the inside of those who have made room for Him. We understand through repentance - (turning from sin and turning to God), and water baptism in Jesus' name, we are prepared to receive this great gift. What happens when the Holy Spirit lives inside of us and helps us daily? This is the question we will try to answer through the verses we study today. Power and boldness come into the life of everyone who receives the gift of the Holy Spirit, their life will never be the same!

1. Read John 7:37-39.

    c.   (v. 37) What does Jesus want us to do?

    _____

    d.   (v. 38) What will be the result?

    _____

    e.   (v. 39) According to this verse, what do "rivers of living water" represent?

    _____

    _____

2. Who do you think qualifies according to scripture to receive the Holy Spirit?

☐ Just good people who attend church regularly.

☐ Pastors, preachers and missions workers.

☐ Anyone who believes in Jesus and repents of their sins.

3. Why do you think it is necessary for you to experience the baptism of the Holy Spirit in your life?

_____

_____

4. In Acts 8:14-17 the Samaritans received the word of God through the preaching of Phillip. They believed, miracles were happening and there was joy in the city. So why did Peter and John go to them?

a. (v. 15) _____

b. (v. 17) What did Peter and John do?

_____

_____

c. (v. 17) What happened next?

_____

_____

5. In Acts 10:44-48 Cornelius was listening to Peter
    share the good news of the Gospel of Jesus
    Christ. What happened next?

    _____

    _____

    _____

    _____

6. How did the Jews (they of the circumcision) know
    that the Gentiles had received the Holy Ghost?

    _____

7. Look closely at Acts 19:1-6. What question did
    Paul ask John's disciple's at Ephesus?

    _____

8. What specific things do you notice from Acts 19
    that are similar to Acts chapters 2, 8 and 10?
    (Check all that apply)

_____ People are being baptized in Jesus' Name.

_____ Laying on of hands, people receive the Holy Ghost.

_____ When people receive the Holy Ghost they speak in tongues

9. What does Matthew 5:6 say are necessary ingredients for being filled?

_____ and _____

10. Read Luke 11:13.

   a. What does the Father want to give you?

   _____

   b. What must you do?

   _____

God is waiting on you. He wants to give you the Holy Spirit, His precious gift.

Let's review the steps we have uncovered in the scriptures for receiving the Holy Spirit:

A.   Hunger and Thirst after God with all your heart.

B.   Repent of your sins and turn to God.

C.	Yield your life to Jesus and hold nothing back.

D.	Pray and ask Jesus to fill you with the precious gift of the Holy Spirit.

E.	Know that God wants to fill you, worship and praise Him in advance.

F.	As you are worshipping Him, He will give you new words to speak and the Holy Spirit will come and live inside you.

The changes you will notice once you have received the Holy Ghost:

- You will speak in tongues and afterwards pray while speaking in tongues, and it will lift your spirit and build you up. (1 Corinthians 14:4, Acts 2:4, 10:46, 19:6).
- You will have a greater desire to live holy before the Lord.
- You will receive power to be His witness (Acts 1:8).
- You will be bolder and more courageous in your witnessing for Jesus (Acts 4:31).
- You will have an increased hunger for the Word of God (Matthew 5:6).

The Baptism of the Holy Spirit is an essential part of the Biblical plan of salvation.

Week 3 - CHARACTER OVER COMFORT
(Days 13-18)

You are doing wonderful! This week of study will be most interesting. You will learn the devil's plan for your life and how you can defeat him. Stay faithful this week and watch God do the miraculous in your life. Once again complete the assignment below and check the appropriate box.

☐ Memory verses

"Therefore, submit to God. Resist the devil and he will flee from you." James 4:7 (NKJV)

"Blessed are the pure in heart, for they shall see God." Matthew 5:8 (NKJV)

☐ Church Attendance

Church Attended _____

How many times church attended _____

☐ Met with Prayer Partner

☐ Prayer Requests

_____

_____

☐ Answered Prayers

_____

_____

What Does God Want?

God wants a close, personal relationship with you. He loves you more than you could ever imagine. His aim is to help you become more like Him every day. He desires to be your closest friend, Lord and Master. In fact, God wants every area of your heart.

1. Romans 8:29 reveals a portion of God's plan for your life. What is it?

   _____

   _____

2. Explain what that means to you?

   _____

   _____

3. According to Romans 6:13, what does God not want you to do and what does He *desire* for you to do?

   _____

   _____

4. Pride is one of the reasons we do not surrender our life to the Lord. Why do you think God has a problem with pride?

   _____

   _____

5. Read Psalm 51:16,17.

   a. What sacrifices will God not reject?

   _____

   _____

   b. What does it mean to have a broken and contrite spirit?

   _____

   _____

   c. How can we become broken and contrite?

   _____

   _____

6. Examine Isaiah 57:15 and list what God says He will do to and for the one who is broken and contrite.

   _____

   _____

   _____

7. What does Paul say in Romans 12:1, 2 that you should and should not do? List them.

   a. (v.1) _____

b. (v. 2) _____

(v. 2) _____

8. According to Matthew 22:37, what does Jesus want
you to do?

_____

_____

What the Devil?

Yes, there really is a literal devil. He is not just a made up character by the church or Hollywood to try and scare people. According to the teachings of the New Testament, the devil is subject to the name of Jesus. There is no need to fear him. However, we should not underestimate him or his power. He is a formidable foe. If you apply the lessons learned in this study, you will understand the enemy of your soul better and be poised for victory.

"The devil and me, we don't agree;
I hate him and he hates me."
Salvation Army Hymn

1. Why was Satan kicked out of heaven? (Isaiah 14:12-14)

_____

_____

2. In Genesis 3:1-5, Satan deceived Eve. How did he do this?

_____

_____

"The devil always leaves a stink behind him."
Author Unknown

3. Examine 2 Corinthians 11:3. How did Satan convince Eve?

_____

65

4. Read 1 Peter 5:8, 9.

    a. (v. 8) What are we instructed to do?

    b. (v. 8) Peter describes the devil as what?

    c. (v. 8) What does he want to do with you?

    d. (v. 9) What action must we take to insure that doesn't happen?

5. Explain James 4:7 in your own words.

"If you don't open the door to the devil, he goes away."

6.   What do the following verses tell you about Satan?

    a.   John 10:10

    _____

    _____

    b.   2 Corinthians 4:3-4

    _____

    _____

    c.   John 8:44

    _____

    _____

    d.   2 Corinthians 11:14

    _____

    _____

7.   How has the devil tried to destroy you or someone you know?

    _____

    _____

8. Examine Ephesians 6:10-18. What instruction does verse 11 give us and why?

_____

_____

Define "wiles."

_____

_____

• *Go ahead and praise Jesus that He is your Savior, your name is written in the Lamb's Book of Life and that you are confirmed by the Holy Ghost.*

Victory Over the Devil

Before you started making your move toward God, the devil didn't worry about you. Now that you are a Christ-follower, he is very upset. The Bible calls the devil your "adversary" (1 Peter 5:8). He is out to get you. Nothing would please him more than for you to mess up, fail God and feel badly about it. However, the good news is that Jesus defeated him on the cross and because of Christ's victory, you can overcome any attack from the enemy.

1. According to Luke 8:12, what does Satan want to do to the person who hears the good news about Jesus?

   _____

   _____

2. According to this scripture, who is hell prepared for? Matthew 25:41

   _____

   _____

3. Because of the death, burial and resurrection, what did Jesus do to Satan? Colossians 2:15

   _____

   _____

4. What future can the devil look forward to? Revelation 20:10

   _____

_____

5. Read Luke 9:1, 2. What specifically did Jesus give to his disciples?

    _____

    _____

6. In Luke 10:17, the seventy disciples that Jesus sent out to preach the Good News came back to him with a remarkable report. What was that report?

    _____

    _____

7. What was Jesus' comment back to them? Luke 10:18

    _____

    _____

8. In Luke 10:19, what did Jesus give to His followers?

    _____

    _____

9. Do you believe you have the same authority and power that the early disciples had?

    _____Yes _____ No. Explain your answer.

_____

_____

10. Read Mark 16:14-18. Jesus instructed His disciples to go and preach the gospel. He also said that certain signs would follow them. What are those signs?

_____

_____

1. Because Jesus lives on the inside of you, now you have power over all the works of the enemy.

2. Exercise that authority and don't be afraid. You are the light of the world!

I'M SO TEMPTED

Within the last 24 hours you have been tempted to sin and disobey God. Today, this study will help you understand the purpose of temptation and reveal God's plan of escape to you. Without God's help and a good understanding of temptation, you will continually fall and make mistakes. Today will encourage you to walk in victory and resist temptation every time. God says in His Word that you are "more than a conqueror." ***Romans 8:37***

1. The Bible clearly states that God doesn't tempt us. Where do the temptations you face come from? James 1:13-15.

    a. (v. 14) _____

    b. (v. 14) _____

2. The Bible lists three main types of temptations in 1 John 2:16. List them in a Bible character who gave in to that particular temptation.

Temptation	**Bible Character**
the _____ of the _____	_____
the _____ of the _____	_____
the _____ of the _____	_____

3. Read 1 Corinthians 10:13 closely.

a. According to the above verse, are others experiencing the same temptations that you are facing? _____ Yes _____ No

b. What will God be to you when you face temptations?

_____

_____

c. List two things God will do for you while you are being tempted.

_____

_____

d. In your own words, what does this verse say to you?

_____

_____

"Flee temptation and leave no forwarding address!"

4. Study 2 Samuel 11:1-4. What could King David have done to avoid committing adultery with Bathsheba? In other words, how could he have "escaped?"

_____

_____

5. Give a recent example of being tempted and yielding to the temptation. Then identify the "exit" door that God provided for you, but you failed to walk through it.

_____

_____

6. Read Genesis 39:7-12.

   a. How did Joseph respond to this temptation? Genesis 39:7-12

   _____

   _____

   b. What can you learn from his example?

   _____

   _____

"It is easier to stay out than to get out."
Mark Twain

7. Read Matthew 4:1-11. After Jesus' baptism He was led into the wilderness for a time of prayer. While there, the devil came and tempted him. How did Jesus respond to the Devil's temptations?

   _____

   _____

8. Given the above example of Jesus, why do you think it is important to meditate and memorize the Word of God?

_____

_____

9. Read Psalm 119:11. What does this mean to you now?

_____

_____

- *Thank the Lord that according to the Bible there is no temptation that you cannot overcome.*

- *Ask him to help you defeat the temptations you are facing right now. Remember, God is faithful!*

POWER OVER SIN

You already know that the devil is your enemy and is out to get you, but did you know that he has a plan for getting you to mess your life up? It is called SIN. You are confronted every day with opportunities to compromise your relationship with God. These scriptures will reveal the devil's plan for your life when it comes to sin.

1. When Cain's offering was refused by God, Cain became angry and jealous of his brother Abel. Read Genesis 4:7.

    a. What position did sin take in Cain's life?

    _____

    _____

    b. What was it doing there? In other words, what did it want? (v. 7)

    _____

    _____

    c. How should you deal with sin? (v.7)

    _____

    _____

2. List three temptations you know are at your heart's door.

    a. _____

b. _____

c. _____

3. Sin has a purpose. According to Romans 6:12, what specifically would sin like to do in your life?

_____

_____

4. What are you instructed to do with your body?

Romans 6:13, 14

_____

_____

Romans 12:1

_____

_____

5. Why do you think it is important to present your body to God?

_____

_____

6. How did the believers overcome Satan in Revelation 12:11?
   a. _____

   b. _____

7. How can you apply Revelation 12:11 to your life?

_____

_____

8. How does James 4:7 encourage and strengthen you in your battle with sin?

_____

_____

9. What does Romans 8:37 say that you are?

_____

_____

10. According to Philippians 4:13, what promise is recorded for you?

_____

_____

LIVE ABOVE SIN

Sin is not your friend. The devil is your proclaimed enemy. The Bible explains sin's objective for your life. Sin wants to destroy you and your influence. Make a commitment today not to let sin live and control your life

1. James 1:14, 15 shows us how sin gets into our lives and its ultimate objective.

    a. What do you do to cause temptations to come your way? (v. 14)

    _____

    b. Who do you think does the "enticing?"

    _____

    c. What happens when you yield to temptation?

    _____

    d. According to verse 15, is it true that sin wants to "grow" and be "more influential" in your life? _____ Yes _____ No

    e. What is sin's ultimate desire for you? (v. 15)

    _____

    _____

2. It is possible to live above sin? (in victory over sin). What does 1 John 5:4, 5 mean to you?

_____

_____

3. In Psalm 119:11, what can you do in order not to sin?

_____

_____

4. What steps can you take in order to activate Psalm 119:11 in your life?

_____

_____

5. Match the following:

_____ Romans 8:2

_____ Romans 8:31

_____ Romans 8:6

_____ Romans 8:13

_____ Romans 8:7

a. "If you live according to the Spirit you put to death the deeds of the body."

b. "To be spiritually minded is life and peace."

c. "Jesus has made me free from the law of sin and death."

d. "The carnal mind is enmity against God."

e. "If God be for us, who can be against us?"

6. Read John 8:31, 32.

   a. What shall make you free?

   _____

   b. According to verse 31, what is the "truth?"

   _____

   _____

7. What instructions did Jesus give the woman in John 8:11?

   _____

   _____

8. What does John 8:12 mean to you?

   _____

   _____

YOU ARE A CHILD OF GOD. ASK GOD FOR THE ABILITY TO WALK HOLY BEFORE HIM AND OTHERS.

Week 4 - LIVING THE BEST LIFE
(Days 19-24)

You are well over half way in your "30 Days to Life" adventure. Don't give up! Be faithful in your daily time with the Lord. Let Him speak to you. The devil wants you to quit. If you don't quit, you can beat the devil in every area of your life and God will get the glory! This is not just a book to read, this guide will give you powerful tools from scripture that you can apply to help you in living the best life possible!

☐ Memory Verse: Mark 8:34
"Whoever desires to come after me, let him deny himself, and take up his cross, and follow me." (NKJV)

☐ Church Attendance
Church Attended _____
How many times did you attend church this week? _____
☐ Met with Prayer Partner

☐ Did you have the opportunity to share Jesus with anybody?
Name(s) _____

☐ Prayer Requests
_____

_____

☐ Answered Prayers
_____

_____

ONLY THE PURE IN HEART

God always looks at our heart. He desires for us to live pure lives before Him and others. Many incredible benefits are promised to those who dare to live with a pure heart. The scriptures we look at today will uncover those special blessings available to us. Get closer to God and He will get closer to you! James 4:7-8

1. Find a dictionary and define "pure."

    _____

    _____

2. According to Matthew 5:8, what does God promise to those who have a pure heart?

    _____

    _____

3. Why do you think it is important to live a pure life before those who do not know Jesus like you do?

    _____

    _____

"A holy life will produce the deepest impression. Lighthouses blow no horns, they only shine."
Dwight L. Moody

4. What does Psalm 24:3-5 say will be the benefit for those who live pure before God?

    _____

> *A holy man is not one who cannot sin.*
> *A holy man is one who will not sin.*
> A.W. Tozer

5. Match the following from 1 Corinthians 6:15-20:

_____ Temple of the Holy Spirit   a. Verse 17

_____ Flee from sexual   b. Verse 19

immorality   c. Verse 16

_____ Holy Spirit who is in you   d. Verse 18

_____ Glorify God with your   e. Verse 20

body

_____ Shall become one flesh

6. Read 2 Corinthians 7:1

    a. What are we to cleanse ourselves from?

    _____

    _____

    b. What are we to perfect?

    _____

    _____

7. As we can tell, God is serious about purity. In Ephesians 5:3-5, list what is not appropriate for the child of God.

_____

_____

8. According to these passages of Scripture, what can you do to please the Lord

1 Peter 1:22 _____

1 Peter 2:11 _____

9. What should be our relationship with those who are not concerned with pleasing and obeying God? Proverbs 4:14, 15

_____

_____

10. Ephesians 4:22, 23 gives you some helpful advice. What is it?

_____

_____

11. Look closely at 1 John 2:15, 16.

What are we not to love?

_____

a. List the three things that are in the world.

i. _____

ii. _____

iii. _____

b. In your own words, list several things that might be considered "of the world."

_____

_____

The temptations you face are very difficult to overcome, but remember Philippians 4:13!

Finally, Read Psalm 51:10. Stop and ask God to do the same in you! Now write how you feel.

_____

_____

I'VE GOT TO TELL SOMEBODY!

Do you find it difficult to keep a juicy secret? Doesn't it drive you crazy until you are able tell someone? Life with Jesus is the best-kept secret in the world. You have probably been feeling strong urges to tell others about Jesus. This is His way of reaching to others through you. Don't forget that Jesus wants to do the same in others as He did in you.

1. What is the necessary ingredient in order to become an effective witness for Jesus? Acts 1:8

_____

_____

2. Read 2 Corinthians 5:17-20.

   a. What did Jesus do for us? (v. 17, 18)

   _____

   _____

   b. What ministry do you have? (v. 18)

   _____

   _____

   c. What has Christ committed to you? (v. 19)

   _____

   _____

91

d. Now that you are saved, you are now what? (v. 20)

_____

_____

e. What does this mean to you?

_____

_____

3. Everybody has a story to tell. When witnessing to your friends or even strangers, you can tell them what your life was like before Jesus, how you came to know Jesus and what He has done in your life since you turned it over to Him.

In John 9 Jesus healed a blind man. Find the verse in the story that describes the three components above.

a. Life before Jesus, verse _____

b. How he met Jesus, verse _____

c. The change in his life after meeting Jesus, verse

_____

d. How did the blind man describe his encounter with Jesus? (v. 25)

_____

_____

4. In your own words, explain why you think it is
    important to tell others about Jesus?

    _____

    _____

5. According to 1 Peter 3:15, how should we live?
    Check the appropriate answer or answers.

    _____ a. Ready to sing

    _____ b. Ready to teach

    _____ c. Ready to go to church

    _____ d. Ready to witness

6. Read 2 Corinthians 4:3-4 carefully.

    a. How can we *VEIL* the Gospel?

        _____

        _____

    b. What happens to those we never tell about
        Jesus? (v. 3)

        _____

        _____

    c. Who is the "god of this world?" (v. 4)

        _____

d. What is he trying to do? (v. 4)

_____

_____

e. What does God want to happen to your friends? (v. 4, 6)

_____

_____

7. What does Proverbs 11:30 say about the one who wins souls?

_____

_____

8. According to Jesus in Matthew 28:19-20, what things are we supposed to be doing?

_____

_____

9. In Acts 1:8, what did Jesus say we would become after receiving the Holy Ghost?

_____

_____

10. List some people in your life to whom God would have you witness.

_____

_____

- *Right now, ask God to prepare their hearts to receive Him.*

- *Furthermore, ask Him to give you the power and boldness to share Christ with them.*

- *Remember, you hold the keys to eternal life-unlock the door of their heart so they can come to Jesus.*

BE FAITHFUL

God desires faithfulness from each and every believer. When you are faithful, you are committed all the way to the end. There is nothing more honorable than faithfulness. When you are loyal and committed to God, He will bless you abundantly in return. Oftentimes, the cares and temptations of this life will try to pull your loyalty in the opposite direction. However, resist compromise and stay committed to the One who laid down His very life for you.

1. According to Psalm 31:23, what will God do to the faithful?

   _____

   _____

2. What will God do if you are faithful to him all the days of your life? Revelation 2:10.

   _____

   _____

3. What is God looking for on the earth?

   2 Chronicles 16:9 _____

   Psalm 101:6 _____

4. According to Luke 9:62, what does Jesus say about unfaithfulness?

   _____

   _____

97

"As you are faithful this one thing is certain, the Lord will show you great and mighty things that you know not now."
Stanley Frodsham

5. What is the benefit of faithfulness? See Proverbs 28:20.

    _____

    _____

6. What does God expect from His children? 1 Corinthians 4:2.

    _____

    _____

7. What does Jesus require from those who wish to follow Him? Matthew 16:24.

    _____

    _____

8. Read Proverbs 13:17 carefully. Describe the difference between a *wicked messenger* and a *faithful ambassador.*

    Wicked Messenger _____

    Faithful Ambassador _____

9. Describe God's servant Caleb. What did God like so much about him? Numbers 14:24.

_____

_____

10. Study Matthew 25:14-30.

    a. (vv. 21, 23) How did Jesus reward faithfulness?

_____

_____

    b. (vv. 28-30) How did Jesus say unfaithfulness will be rewarded?

_____

_____

- *Ask God for the power and strength to remain faithful to Him.*

- *Pray for the strength to resist all temptations that would cause you to compromise your commitment to Jesus.*

- *Remember, God desires faithfulness. He loves it when His children are faithful to Him! BE FAITHFUL!*

BE A DISCIPLE

There is a big difference between a believer and a disciple. A disciple is one who not only has a relationship with God, but is teachable and willing to receive instruction from Him. Believers, on the other hand, are satisfied with the status quo of knowing who God is, and no more. As you can tell, the difference between the two lies in the intensity of passion and hunger within a person. It is possible to be a believer, and never reach the ultimate level of living as a disciple. Are you willing to settle for a general relationship with the Lord or do you desire a deeper relationship, like that between a loving father and child?

The Greek translation for the word "disciple" in the New Testament is "learner." The term refers to one who has learned certain principles from another and maintains them on another's authority. Simply put, disciples go beyond mere confession to a complete change in lifestyle, priorities and passions. Jesus is looking for modern-day *disciples!*

1. What did Jesus say to Matthew that changed his life? See Matthew 9:9.

    _____

    _____

2. Check out Luke 14:26-27. What are some issues Jesus lists, that hinder people from becoming disciples?

    a. v.26 _____

    b. v. 27 _____

3. What did Jesus say should characterize His disciples?

John 8:31 _____

John 13:34-35 _____

John 15:8 _____

4. Read Luke 9:23-26.

    a. Jesus gave three requirements to be his disciple. What are they?

  i. _____

  ii. _____

  iii. _____

    b. What does verse 24 mean to you?

_____

_____

5. In your opinion, what is the difference between a Christian and a Disciple?

_____

_____

6. Check the statements below that describe a true disciple.

_____ Sets his heart to please others

_____ Sets his heart to please Jesus all the time

_____ Will suffer if need be to follow Christ

_____ Will obey the Bible when it is convenient

_____ Longs to tell others about Jesus

7. Check out Proverbs 4:23. As a disciple it is important to keep our hearts pure. Why?

_____

_____

BEAR FRUIT

The closer we are to God, the more we will learn to live fruitful, productive lives. It is important to God that our lives bear fruit for His glory. As you study this lesson, the heart of God will be revealed to you. You will begin to recognize the significance God places on this important part of your Christian walk. The more you grow in your relationship with Him, the more He will do in your life and through your life.

1. Take some time to read and meditate on John 15:1-8.

    a. (v. 1) Jesus is the _____. God is the
        _____.

    b. (v. 2) What will God do to the branch that does not bear fruit? _____

    c. (v. 2) What will God do to the branch that bears fruit? Why?

        _____

        _____

    d. (v. 5) What must you do in order to bear fruit for Jesus?

        _____

        _____

    e. (v. 7) What must you do in order to have your prayers answered?

        _____

105

f.   (v. 8) How is God glorified?

_____

_____

2.   According to Psalm 1:1-3, what will cause you to bear fruit on a consistent basis?

_____

_____

3.   In your own words, explain John 15:16.

_____

_____

4.   For whom should we bear fruit, according to Romans 7:4?

_____

_____

5.   Describe Jesus' warning in Matthew 3:10.

_____

_____

6.   List the nine fruits of the Spirit as found in Galatians 5:22, 23.

_____

7. What helps us tell the difference between someone who is a real Christian and someone who is not? Matthew 7:16, 20.

_____

_____

8. Match the following:

_____ Fruit worthy of repentance   a. Romans 6:22

_____ Good tree-no evil fruit   b. Luke 3:8

_____ You are known by your   c. Matthew 7:18

fruit   d. Ephesians 5:9

_____ Fruit unto holiness   e. Luke 6:44

_____ Fruit of the Spirit

Paul told his friends to be what, according to Philippians 1:11?

_____

_____

- *Ask God every morning, when you wake up, to help you bear fruit for His glory.*

- *Commit yourself to His service and watch how fruit will begin to grow in your life.*

107

TAMING THE TONGUE

The tongue is the most destructive member of our bodies and may even be the enemy's greatest weapon. With the power to destroy relationships, homes, and careers, the damage it leaves behind is often far too difficult to undo. This study will help you understand how God wants us to use our mouth and use our tongue to encourage and bless others, rather than allow it to tear down and destroy.

1. Read James 3:3-12.
    a. What do verses 3-6 say about your tongue?

    _____

    _____

    b. Paraphrase verse 8:

    _____

    _____

    c. According to verses 9-12, what should not be happening with your tongue?

    _____

    _____

2. According to Ephesians 4:29, what kind of things should come out of your mouth?

    _____

3. What does your speech reveal about your heart? Matthew 12:34-35.

_____

_____

4. How can you put Colossians 4:6 into practice?

_____

_____

5. What does Proverbs 12:19 say about your mouth?

_____

_____

"Your life will move in the direction of your words."
Mike Murdock

6. How much power do your words have? Proverbs 18:21.

_____

_____

7. Match the following:

_____ Refrain his tongue from evil   a. Proverbs 15:4

_____ Tongue of the wise is health   b. 1 Peter 3:10

_____ Guards his mouth   c. Proverbs 13:3

_____ A deceitful tongue   d. Psalm 120:2

_____ Tree of knowledge   e. Proverbs 12:18

8. How can you apply the truth of Proverbs 15:1 to your every day life?

_____

_____

- *Ask God right now to help you guard the words of your mouth.*
- *Pray for the strength to speak only words of life and blessing to others.*

Week 5 - MY RESPONSIBILITY & REWARD
(Days 25-30)

Just six days remaining. Congratulations! You did it. The goal of this book is to help you see that the answer for all of life's questions can be found in God's Word. We hope you have been encouraged to follow Christ daily. No doubt there have been a lot of changes in your life over the recent days. This is just the beginning. Jesus wants to make You more like Him every day. Let Him have His way in your life!

☐ Memory Verse: Matthew 6:33
"But seek first the kingdom of God and his righteousness, and all these things shall be added to you." (NKJV)

☐ Church Attendance
Church Attended _____

How many times did you attend church this week? _____

☐ Have you joined a church? _____ yes _____ not yet

☐ Met with Prayer Partner

☐ Did you have the opportunity to share Jesus with anybody?

Name(s) _____

☐ Prayer Requests

_____

_____

☐ Answered Prayers

_____

_____

LET IT GO!

You are most like Christ when you make the decision to show mercy and forgiveness to those who have hurt you. Forgiveness is God's best for your life. In this chapter, you will learn about the importance of letting go of bitterness and hurt, by forgiving those who have harmed you.

1. According to 1 Peter 4:8, what will sincere love do?

_____

_____

2. According to Jesus' words in Matthew 6:14-15, what will the Father do if you forgive someone who has wronged you?

_____

_____

   a. (v.14) What will be the result if you refuse to forgive others?

_____

_____

3. How many times are we to forgive someone according to Matthew 18:21-22?

_____

"Forgiveness is the fragrance that the flower leaves on the heel of the one who crushed it." - Mark Twain

4. Read Ephesians 4:32. What three commands are given?

    a. _____

    b. _____

    c. _____

5. Bitterness can overcome a person's heart if he/she fails to forgive. According to Hebrews 12:15, what two things will bitterness do to a person?

    a. _____

    b. _____

6. Read Colossians 3:13. What are we instructed to do and why?

    _____

    _____

7. Check out Romans 12:18-21. What does God want us to do in the following verses?

Verse 18

    _____

    _____

Verse 19

_____

_____

8. What does God say He will do about your situation?
   (v.19)

_____

_____

9. What are we instructed to do to our enemies?

_____

_____

10. How should you overcome the evil that others do to
    you? (v. 21)

_____

_____

- *Take the next few minutes to ask the Holy Spirit to
  reveal the people in your life whom you have not
  yet forgiven.*
- *Now ask God for the ability to release and forgive
  those individuals. You will be set free!*

SERVICE THROUGH LOVE

Jesus' life was an incredible example of service to others. Right before Jesus went to the cross, He and His close friends met together for dinner and fellowship. At this event, Jesus took a basin of water and a towel and washed His disciples' feet. He plainly set an example for us. It is by His Spirit and His love in our hearts that we can serve each other in humility.

1. Look at Matthew 20:26. What does Jesus tell His disciples about greatness?

    _____

    _____

2. Look now at Matthew 20:27. What did Jesus say about wanting to be first?

    _____

    _____

3. Read Matthew 20:28. What did Jesus reveal to us about His own life?

    _____

    _____

"Do all the good you can, by all the means you can, and all the ways you can, and all the places you can, at all the times you can, to all the people you can, as long as you ever can." - John Wesley

4. In what ways could you apply the teaching of Jesus regarding service to your life right now?

_____

_____

5. What instruction do you receive from Galatians 5:13?

_____

_____

6. How are we to love each other? Galatians 5:14

_____

_____

"Life is a lot like tennis-he who serves best seldom loses."

7. Read Galatians 6:9, 10.

   a. What does God promise if we endure and do good to others?

   _____

   _____

b. Write in your own words how you can put
    verse 10 into practice.

_____

_____

"God can do tremendous things through people
who don't care who gets the credit."

8. In Mark 10:45 Jesus reveals His purpose for coming
    to the earth. State that purpose.

_____

_____

9. Below is your serving list. Write down the names of
    three people whom God would have you serve. Your
    goal is to be a blessing to them. In the space provided,
    write how you can best serve and bless them.

Name # 1 _____

My action for blessing

_____

_____

Name # 2 _____

My action for blessing

_____

_____

Name # 3 _____

My action for blessing

_____

_____

- *Thank God right now for the opportunity to serve others.*

- *Jesus set the example for us.*

- *Ask Him for the Strength and understanding of how to bless others.*

GOD'S PROMISE ABOUT MONEY

God has a lot to say about money. There are 500 verses on prayer, 500 verses on faith and over 2,000 verses that address the issue of money. Did you know 20% of the Bible addresses money and money management? In fact, 16 out of Jesus' 38 parables deal with money. It is important to understand God's promises about money and His direction for your finances. The devil doesn't want you to prosper and so keeping you bound financially is one of his greatest weapons. According to theologians, the tithe was established four hundred years before the law was given to Moses. It is God's will that all of His children bring a tithe to their place of worship. What is a tithe? A tithe is 10% of your income. This is God's way of seeing if your heart and life completely belong to Him. It is true that finances are one of the hardest things to surrender to God. When God is in charge of your finances, then the chances are He has ALL of you. In the questions to follow, you will realize the importance of obeying God in this area of your life. The rewards are outstanding. Be ready to watch God work in your life and finances like never before.

1. Psalm 35:27 reveals the heart of God about money and you. What is it?

    _____

    _____

2. Read Deuteronomy 8:18.
    a. What does God empower us to do?

    _____

    _____

b.   Why?

_____

_____

3.   So is God against you becoming blessed financially?

_____ yes _____ no

"Satan is not nearly as concerned with driving you backwards as he is with CONTAINING you where you are, and KEEPING you from getting where God wants you to go." - John Avanzini

4.   Write Proverbs 10: 22 in your own words.

_____

_____

5.   Read 1 Timothy 6:9-10.

    a.   (v. 9) What does Timothy say will happen to those who use all of their time and energy to become rich?

_____

_____

    b.   (v. 10) What is the "root of all evil?"

_____

6. According to Proverbs 22:7, why is borrowing money not a good idea?

_____

_____

   a. Have you ever borrowed money and realized later that you made a mistake? Explain:

_____

_____

7. What does Luke 12:15 tell us about a man's life?

_____

_____

8. Read Matthew 6:33.

   a. What should be our highest priority?

_____

_____

   b. What will be the result?

_____

_____

9. Read Proverbs 3:9-10.

    a. In your own words, what does verse 9 mean to you?

    _____

    _____

    b. What will be the benefit? (v. 10)

    _____

    _____

10. What stands out to you the most about Proverbs 11:24-25?

    _____

    _____

11. Read Malachi 3:8-11.

    a. (v.8) if one fails to tithe his\her income, what does God say they are doing to Him?

    _____

    _____

    b. (v. 9) what does God say will be the result of not tithing?

    _____

    _____

c. In your opinion, what does this mean to you?

_____

_____

d. (v. 10) what are we commanded to do and why?

_____

_____

e. (v. 10) what will God do for us if we give 10% of our income to Him?

_____

_____

f. (v. 10) does God want you to "try" or "test" Him in this area of Your life?

☐ Yes   ☐ No

12. What does God promise us if we are faithful in our giving? Philippians 4:19

_____

_____

13. Read 2 Corinthians 9:6-8.

a. (v.6) what happens if you give little?

_____

_____

b. (v.6) what happens if you give much?

_____

_____

c. (v.7) what kind of giver does God love?

_____

_____

d. (v. 8) what is God able to do for you after you give unto Him?

_____

_____

• *This Sunday and every Sunday you have the opportunity to bring your tithes to the Lord. Trust God. Be strong and have faith.*

• *God will not fail you. In fact, you will be amazed at how God comes through for you. He will truly open the windows of heaven over your life.*

• ***Wealth and Wisdom – read Proverbs 8:12-18***

LOVING OTHERS

When we truly love others like Christ loved us, something incredible happens. The power of love transforms lives that once had no hope. There are around 7 billion people on the earth and millions of those people have never heard a clear presentation of the gospel. This breaks the heart of God. He desires everyone to know Him. The question is: "Will you love others with Jesus love and share His Gospel with them?"

1. For whom did Jesus come and die? John 3:16

   _____

   _____

2. What motivated Jesus to manifest Himself as a man on earth?

   _____

   _____

3. Matthew 28:19-20 and Mark 16:15 are known as the "Great Commission." As Christians, what does God expect you to do?

   _____

   _____

""Because God has made us for Himself, our hearts are restless until they rest in Him."
~ Augustine of Hippo

4. When Jesus saw the masses of humanity, what did He ask His disciples to pray? Matthew 9:36-38

_____

_____

5. What did Jesus mean in the following passages? John 17:18 and 20:21

John 17: 18 _____

John 20:21 _____

6. Read John 4:35. What does this reveal about the condition of the world?

_____

_____

7. Usually, the last words someone speaks on earth reveal their heart and desire. What does Acts 1:8 reveal about Jesus' heart and desire for your life?

_____

_____

8. According to 2 Thessalonians 1:8-9 and Revelation 20:12, 15, why must we move quickly to tell the world about Jesus?

_____

9. Read 2 Peter 3:9. What does this say about the Father's heart?

_____

_____

10. In the next 18 months, what is your plan to go into all the world with Jesus' love?

_____

_____

QUESTION:

- *How many people will be in heaven because of your influence?*

HEAVEN, MY ETERNAL HOME

The word of God has a lot to say about heaven. One day each of us will take our last breath here on this earth. Our last breath here will be our first breath in heaven. Think about it. By going to the cross Jesus has already prepared a place for you in heaven (John 14:1-3). Can you imagine how beautiful it is going to be? These scriptures will encourage you as you look forward to your eternal home with Jesus.

1. What does this verse reveal about heaven? 1 Corinthians 2:9

_____

_____

2. According to Proverbs 14:32, what blessing do the righteous have when they die?

_____

_____

3. Why do you think Psalm 116:15 is true?

_____

_____

"This world is the land of the dying; the next is the land of the living."
Tryon Edwards

4. What will God do when you get to heaven? Revelation 21:4

_____

_____

    a. According to the above verse, what will not be allowed into heaven?

    _____

    _____

5. According to 1 John 3:2, what will we be like in heaven?

_____

_____

6. What will take place after a person dies? Hebrews 9:27

_____

_____

7. In your own words, explain the truth of John 11:25, 26.

_____

134

"There is no death. Only a change of worlds."
Chief Seattle

8. What did John see in Revelation 21:1, 2?

_____

_____

9. What do you think will be the greatest things about heaven? List at least three.

_____

_____

_____

_____

10. Read Hebrews 12:1-2.

    a. Who do you think is looking at us from that cloud of witnesses?

    _____

    _____

b. Because we have a heavenly audience, what should we do with the rest of our lives on earth?

_____

_____

USING MY SPIRITUAL GIFTS

By now, you might have heard the phrase "spiritual gifts." Maybe you do not even know what those words mean. The goal on this final day is to help you understand how God has gifted you and the church to carry out His purposes upon earth.

1. What does Ephesians 4:7-8 say Jesus did when He ascended?

   _____

   _____

2. Read Ephesians 4:11-16.

   a. (v. 11) List five of the gifts He gave.

   _____

   _____

   _____

   _____

   _____

   b. (vv. 12-16) List at least four reasons why God gave the above gifts to the body of Christ.

   _____

137

_____

_____

_____

3. Read 1 Corinthians 12:1-11.

    a. (vv. 8-10) List the gifts that are discussed.

    _____

    _____

    b. (v. 11) Who distributes the gifts?

    _____

    _____

4. According to Romans 12:6, will everyone have the
    same spiritual gift?

    _____ yes _____ no

5. List the gifts that are mentioned in Romans 12:6-8

    _____

    _____

6. How should we use the gifts that we have received
    from God? 1 Peter 4:10

    _____

7. What are we to desire? 1 Corinthians 12:31

_____

_____

8. In your opinion, what do you believe to be the most desirable gifts?

_____

_____

9. What gift(s) have you seen active or operating in your life?

_____

_____

- *Pray now and thank God for the gift(s) He has given you.*

- *Ask Him for the wisdom on when and how to use those gifts.*

- *God will give you the exact gift when you need it to bring glory and honor to His name.*

CONGRATULATIONS
ON COMPLETING

"30 DAYS TO LIFE"

KEEP GROWING
IN GOD'S WORD EVERY DAY!

I AM GOING TO MAKE IT

Right now you may feel that the devil is hard after you. In fact, he is. He wants you to go back to the old lifestyle you once lived. A part of you may want to give up. Even quit. However, you know that you have come too far to quit now. Jesus has done so much in you—don't walk away from Him. If you will endure the race, it will be worth the sacrifice. Listen, you are being tested. That's right. You are going through a time of testing, but you can pass the test. Press on!

1. What does Paul's statement and Galatians 6:9 tell us we should do during times of testing?

   _____

   _____

2. What is God's promise to you if you endure?

   _____

   _____

3. According to Romans 5:3-4, what do hard times produce?

   _____

   _____

"By perseverance the snail reached the ark."
Charles H. Spurgeon

4. What instruction does the believer receive from 1 Corinthians 15:58?

_____

_____

5. Read Hebrews 10:23.

   a. What are we encouraged to do?

   _____

   _____

   b. Why?

   _____

   _____

6. James 1:2-4 gives us reasons why we must not quit when things get tough. List those reasons below.

   _____

   _____

   "The human spirit is never finished when it is defeated...it is finished when it surrenders." — Ben Stein

7. What must we do? 2 Timothy 2:3

   _____

8. How can 2 Corinthians 4:17, 18 help you when you are going through difficult times?

_____

_____

9. What are we instructed to do when we want to quit? 1 Timothy 6:12

_____

_____

10. Read Proverbs 24:10. What does this mean to you?

_____

_____

**"The nose of the bulldog is slanted backwards so he can continue to breathe without letting go." —
Winston Churchill**

- *If you will endure and continue with Jesus, you will overcome.*

- *Ask God now for the ability to persevere*

- *Remember, you never win by quitting. There is too much at stake.*

- *Stay the course and fight the good fight of faith!*

INCREASE YOUR FAITH
Part I

1. What does Hebrews 11:1 say faith is?

   _____

   _____

2. Read Romans 10:17. How do we gain faith?

   _____

   _____

3. Keeping Hebrews 11:1 and Romans 10:17 in mind, what are some things you can do to grow your faith in God?

   a. _____

   b. Attend church and listen to the teaching and preaching of His Word

   c. _____

   d. _____

4. Paraphrase Mark 9:23.

   _____

   _____

"It is when active faith dares to believe God to the point of action, that something has to happen."
Kathryn Kuhlman

5. According to Mark 11:24, what does Jesus describe as happening when we pray and believe?

_____

_____

6. As Christians, how should we walk throughout our lives, according to 2 Corinthians 5:7?

_____

_____

7. Examine Romans 4:20-21. Abraham was a man full of faith. What do these verses reveal to us about having faith and trusting in the faithfulness of God?

_____

_____

8. Check out James 5:15.

   a. Discuss what you understand "the prayer of faith" to be.

_____

_____

b. What happens when we pray the prayer of faith?

_____

_____

9. What can hinder you and others from witnessing the power of God at work in your life?

_____

_____

10. Read Luke 18:35-43.

   a. Describe this man's disability and limitations (v. 35)

   _____

   _____

   b. What did he ask Jesus to do? (v. 41)

   _____

   c. What, did Jesus say, healed him? (v. 42)

   _____

"Faith begins where the will of God is known."
F. F. Bosworth

INCREASE YOUR FAITH
(PART 2)

God is moved by our faith more than our needs. Just think about it-everyone has needs. But it is when we exercise our faith that God stops and takes notice of our situation. Start exercising your faith. As you will see in the examples below, it's the best way to get His attention.

1. Check out Mark 5:25-34. In this passage, a woman who had a twelve-year long disease, was miraculously healed. What, did Jesus say, was the reason for her healing?

   (v. 34) _____

2. According to Mark 11:22, in whom should we have faith?

   _____

3. What, did Jesus say, will take place when we exercise our faith? Mark 11:23.

   _____

   _____

"You get faith by studying the word. Study that word until something in you "knows that you know" and that you do not just hope that you know."
Carrie Judd Montgomery

4. Please match the following:

_____ Hebrews 11:30   a. "Without faith it is impossible to please God"

_____ Hebrews 11:39   b. "By faith we understand the world was framed by the word of God"

_____ Hebrews 11:3

    c. "By faith the walls of Jericho fell"

_____ Hebrews 11:6

    d. "They obtained a good testimony through faith"

5. What does your faith help you to accomplish?

_____

_____

6. In Hebrews 4:2 a reason is given for the Israelites not being saved. Give the reason.

_____

_____

YOU DON'T WANT TO MISS THIS:
God has great plans for His children. He is good and desires to bless us with good things. However, in order to receive the promises of God, we must mix His Word with faith. Without faith, we cannot receive His blessing and promises in our lives.

7. Read Ephesians 2:8, 9. How does one enter into the family of God?

_____

_____

8. What did Jesus mean by what He said in Mark 9:23?

_____

_____

9. List three things you are believing God to do in your life.
   a. _____

   b. _____

   c. _____

> *"We tend to get what we expect."*
> Norman Vincent Peale

10. What reason does the writer in Hebrews 10:23 gives us regarding why we can continue to believe God, even when things don't seem to be going our way?

_____

_____

- *This week look for opportunities to increase your faith.*
- *Let the Word of God get inside of your spirit. This will build your faith.*

50557593R10088

Made in the USA
Charleston, SC
26 December 2015